Born in 1969

By

Kerry Butters.

Born in 1969.

Millennium:	2nd millennium
Centuries:	19th century – **20th century** – 21st century
Decades:	1930s 1940s 1950s – **1960s** – 1970s 1980s 1990s
Years:	1966 1967 1968 – **1969** – 1970 1971 1972

1969 (MCMLXIX) was a common year starting on Wednesday (dominical letter E) of the Gregorian calendar, the 1969th year of the Common Era (CE) and *Anno Domini* (AD) designations, the 969th year of the 2nd millennium, the 69th year of the 20th century, and the 10th and last year of the 1960s decade. The year is associated with the first manned landing on the Moon (Apollo 11).

Contents

Events

January

- January 2
  - Australian media baron Rupert Murdoch purchases the largest selling British Sunday newspaper, *The News of the World*.
  - People's Democracy begins a march from Belfast to Derry City, Northern Ireland to gain publicity and to promote its cause.
  - Ohio State defeats USC in the Rose Bowl to win the national title for the 1968 season.
- January 4 – The Government of Spain hands over Ifni to Morocco.
- January 5 – The Soviet Union launches *Venera 5* toward Venus.
- January 6 – The final passenger train traverses the Waverley Line, which subsequently closes to passengers.
- January 10 – the Soviet Union launches *Venera 6* toward Venus.

- January 12
  - *Led Zeppelin*, the first Led Zeppelin album, is released.
  - Martial law is declared in Madrid, as the University is closed and over 300 students are arrested.
  - The New York Jets upset the Baltimore Colts in Super Bowl III, 16-7. Joe Namath is the MVP of the game.
- January 14
  - An explosion aboard the USS *Enterprise* near Hawaii kills 27 and injures 314.
  - The Soviet Union launches *Soyuz 4*.
- January 15 – The Soviet Union launches *Soyuz 5*, which docks with Soyuz 4 for a transfer of crew.
- January 16 – Student Jan Palach sets himself on fire in Prague's Wenceslas Square to protest the Soviet invasion of Czechoslovakia; 3 days later he dies.
- January 18 – In Washington, D.C., the Smithsonian displays the art of Winslow Homer for 6 weeks.
- January 20
  - Richard Milhous Nixon succeeds Lyndon Baines Johnson as the 37th President of the United States of America.

37th President Richard M. Nixon

○

- After 147 years, the last issue of *The Saturday Evening Post* is published (publication resumed in 1971).
- January 26 – Elvis Presley steps into American Studios in Memphis, Tennessee, recording "Long Black Limousine", thus beginning the recording of what becomes his landmark comeback sessions for the albums *From Elvis in Memphis* and *Back in Memphis*. The sessions yield the popular and critically acclaimed singles "Suspicious Minds", "In the Ghetto", and "Kentucky Rain".
- January 27
  - Fourteen men, 9 of them Jews, are executed in Baghdad for spying for Israel.
  - Reverend Ian Paisley, Northern Irish Unionist leader and founder of the Free Presbyterian Church of Ulster is jailed for three months for illegal assembly.

- The present-day Hetch Hetchy Moccasin Powerhouse, rated at 100,000 KVA, is completed and placed in operation.
- January 28 – A blow-out on Union Oil's Platform spills 80,000 to 100,000 barrels of crude oil into a channel and onto the beaches of Santa Barbara County in Southern California, inspiring Wisconsin Senator Gaylord Nelson to organize the first Earth Day in 1970.
- January 30 – The Beatles give their last public performance, filming several tracks on the roof of Apple Records, London.

February

- February 2
  - Two cosmonauts transfer from Soyuz 5 to Soyuz 4 via a spacewalk while the two craft are docked together, the first time such a transfer takes place. The two spacecraft undock. Soyuz 4 will reenter Earth's atmosphere and land February 17 while Soyuz 5 will have a hard landing February 18.
  - Ten paintings are defaced in New York's Metropolitan Museum of Art.
- February 4 – In Cairo, Yasser Arafat is elected Palestine Liberation Organization leader at the Palestinian National Congress.
- February 5 – A huge oil spill off the coast of Santa Barbara, California, closes the city's harbor.
- February 7 – The original Hetch Hetchy Moccasin Powerhouse is removed from service.
- February 8 – The Allende meteorite explodes over Mexico.

- February 8 – The last issue of *The Saturday Evening Post* hits magazine stands.
- February 9 – The Boeing 747 makes its maiden flight.
- February 13 – FLQ terrorists bomb the Stock Exchange in Montreal.
- February 14 – Pope Paul VI issues a motu proprio deleting many names from the Roman calendar of saints (including Valentine, who was celebrated on that day).
- February 17 – Aquanaut Berry L. Cannon dies of carbon dioxide poisoning while attempting to repair the SEALAB III habitat off San Clemente Island, California.
- February 24
  - The *Mariner 6* Mars probe is launched.
  - *Tinker v. Des Moines Independent Community School District*: The U.S. Supreme Court rules that the First Amendment applies to public schools.

March

January 14: Explosion kills 27 on USS *Enterprise*

- March 2
  - In Toulouse, France the first Concorde test flight is conducted.

- Soviet and Chinese forces clash at a border outpost on the Ussuri River.
- March 3
  - In a Los Angeles court, Sirhan Sirhan admits that he killed presidential candidate Robert F. Kennedy.
  - Apollo program: NASA launches *Apollo 9* (James McDivitt, David Scott, Rusty Schweickart) to test the lunar module.
  - The United States Navy establishes the Navy Fighter Weapons School (also known as Top Gun) at Naval Air Station Miramar.
- March 4 – Jim Morrison is arrested in Florida for indecent exposure during a Doors-concert three days earlier.
- March 10
  - In Memphis, Tennessee, James Earl Ray pleads guilty to assassinating Martin Luther King Jr. (he later retracts his guilty plea).
  - The novel *The Godfather* by Mario Puzo is published.
- March 13 – Apollo program: *Apollo 9* returns safely to Earth after testing the Lunar Module.
- March 17
  - The Longhope lifeboat is lost after answering a mayday call during severe storms in the Pentland Firth; the entire crew of 8 die.
  - Golda Meir becomes the first female prime minister of Israel.
- March 18 – Operation Breakfast, the secret bombing of Cambodia, begins.
- March 19

- British paratroopers and Marines land on the island of Anguilla.
- A 385 metres (1,263 ft) tall TV mast at Emley Moor, UK, collapses due to ice build-up.
- March 20 – John Lennon and Yoko Ono are married at Gibraltar, and proceed to their honeymoon "Bed-In" for peace in Amsterdam.
- March 22 – The landmark art exhibition *When Attitudes become Form*, curated by Harald Szeemann, opens at the Kunsthalle Bern in Bern, Switzerland.
- March 29 – The Eurovision Song Contest 1969 is held in Madrid, and results in four co-winners, with 18 votes each, from Spain, the United Kingdom, the Netherlands, and France.
- March 30 – The body of former United States General and President Dwight D. Eisenhower is brought by caisson to the United States Capitol to lie in state in the Capitol Rotunda; Eisenhower had died two days earlier, after a long illness, in the Walter Reed Army Medical Center, Washington, D.C.

April

- April 1 – The Hawker Siddeley Harrier enters service with the Royal Air Force.
- April 4 – Dr. Denton Cooley implants the first temporary artificial heart.
- April 9
  - The Harvard University Administration Building is seized by close to 300 students, mostly members of the

Students for a Democratic Society. Before the takeover ends, 45 will be injured and 184 arrested.

- Fermín Monasterio Pérez is murdered by the ETA in Biscay, Spain; the 4th victim in the name of Basque nationalism.

- April 13 – Queensland: The Brisbane Tramways end service after 84 years of operation.
- April 15 – The EC-121 shootdown incident: North Korea shoots down the aircraft over the Sea of Japan, killing all 31 on board.
- April 20
    - British troops arrive in Northern Ireland to reinforce the Royal Ulster Constabulary.
    - A grassroots movement of Berkeley community members seizes an empty lot owned by the University of California, to begin the formation of "People's Park".
- April 22 – Robin Knox-Johnston becomes the first person to sail around the world solo without stopping.
- April 24 – Recently formed British Leyland launches their first new model, the Austin Maxi in Portugal.
- April 28 – Charles de Gaulle steps down as president of France after suffering defeat in a referendum the day before.

May

- May 10
    - Zip to Zap, a harbinger of the Woodstock Concert, ends with the dispersal and eviction of youths and young adults at Zap, North Dakota by the National Guard.

- The Battle of Dong Ap Bia, also known as Hamburger Hill, begins during the Vietnam War.
- May 13 – May 13 Incident: Race riots occur in Kuala Lumpur, Malaysia.
- May 14 – Colonel Muammar Gaddafi visits Mecca, Saudi Arabia.
- May 15 – An American teenager known as 'Robert R.' dies in St. Louis, Missouri, of a baffling medical condition. In 1984 it will be identified as the first confirmed case of HIV/AIDS in North America.
- May 16 – Venera program: *Venera 5*, a Soviet spaceprobe, lands on Venus.
- May 17 – Venera program: Soviet probe *Venera 6* begins to descend into Venus' atmosphere, sending back atmospheric data before being crushed by pressure.
- May 18 – Apollo program: *Apollo 10* (Tom Stafford, Gene Cernan, John Young) is launched, on the full dress-rehearsal for the Moon landing.
- May 20 – United States National Guard helicopters spray skin-stinging powder on anti-war protesters in California.
- May 21 – *Rosariazo*: Civil unrest breaks out in Rosario, Argentina, following the death of a 15-year-old student.
- May 22 – Apollo program: *Apollo 10*'s lunar module flies to within 15,400 m of the Moon's surface.
- May 25 – *Midnight Cowboy*, an X-rated, Oscar-winning John Schlesinger film, is released.
- May 26
  - The Andean Pact (Andean Group) is established.

- Apollo program: *Apollo 10* returns to Earth, after a successful 8-day test of all the components needed for the upcoming first manned Moon landing.
- May 26–June 2 – John Lennon and Yoko Ono conduct their second Bed-In. The follow-up to the Amsterdam event is held at the Queen Elizabeth Hotel in Montreal, Quebec. Lennon composes and records the song *Give Peace a Chance* during the Bed-In.
- May 29
  - *Cordobazo*: A general strike and civil unrest break out in Córdoba, Argentina.
  - Guided tours begin at the Kremlin and other government sites in Moscow.
- May 30 – Riots in Curaçao mark the start of an Afro-Caribbean civil rights movement on the island.

June

- June 3 – While operating at sea on SEATO maneuvers, the Australian aircraft carrier HMAS *Melbourne* accidentally rams and slices in two the American destroyer USS *Frank E. Evans* in the South China Sea, killing 74 American seamen.
- June 5 – An international communist conference begins in Moscow.
- June 7 – The rock group Blind Faith plays its first gig in front of 100,000 people in London's Hyde Park.
- June 8 – U.S. President Richard Nixon and South Vietnamese President Nguyễn Văn Thiệu meet at Midway Island. Nixon announces that 25,000 U.S. troops will be withdrawn by September.

- June 17 – After a 23-game match, Boris Spassky defeats Tigran Petrosian to become the World Chess Champion in Moscow.
- June 18–June 22 – The National Convention of the Students for a Democratic Society, held in Chicago, collapses, and the Weatherman faction seizes control of the SDS National Office. Thereafter, any activity run from the National Office or bearing the name of SDS is Weatherman-controlled.
- June 20 – Georges Pompidou is elected President of France.
- June 22
  - The Cuyahoga River fire helps spur an avalanche of water pollution control activities resulting in the Clean Water Act, Great Lakes Water Quality Agreement and the creation of the federal Environmental Protection Agency.
  - Judy Garland dies of a drug overdose in her London home.
- June 23 – Warren E. Burger is sworn in as Chief Justice of the United States by retiring Chief Justice Earl Warren.
- June 24 – The United Kingdom and Rhodesia sever diplomatic ties.
- June 28 – The Stonewall riots in New York City mark the start of the modern gay rights movement in the U.S.

July

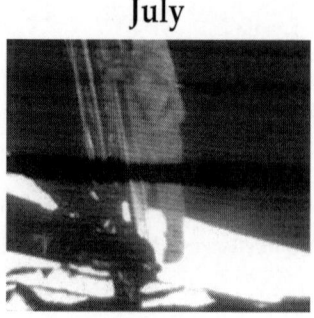

Neil Armstrong descends a ladder to become the first human to step onto the surface of the Moon during Apollo 11

- July 1
    - Charles, Prince of Wales, is invested with his title at Caernarfon.
    - David Simonsen, longterm council member of the European Democratic Education Community was born
- July 3 – Brian Jones, musician and founder of The Rolling Stones, drowns in his swimming pool at his home in Sussex, England.
- July 4 – Michael Mageau and Darlene Ferrin are shot at Blue Rock Springs in California. They are the second (known) victims of the Zodiac Killer. Mageau survives the attack while Ferrin is pronounced dead-on-arrival at Kaiser Foundation Hospital - Richmond.
- July 5 – Tom Mboya, Kenyan Minister of Development, is assassinated.
- July 6 – Francisco Franco orders the closing of the border and communications between Gibraltar and Spain in response to the 1967 Gibraltar sovereignty referendum.

- July 7 – French is made equal to English throughout the Canadian national government.
- July 8 – Vietnam War: The very first U.S. troop withdrawals are made.
- July 10 – Donald Crowhurst's trimaran *Teignmouth Electron* is found drifting and unoccupied. It is assumed that Crowhurst might have committed suicide.
- July 14
  - Football War: After Honduras loses a soccer game against El Salvador, rioting breaks out in Honduras against Salvadoran migrant workers. Of the 300,000 Salvadoran workers in Honduras, tens of thousands are expelled, prompting a brief Salvadoran invasion of Honduras. The OAS works out a cease-fire on July 18, which takes effect on July 20.
  - The Act of Free Choice commences in Merauke, West Irian.
  - The United States' $500, $1,000, $5,000 and $10,000 bills are officially withdrawn from circulation.
- July 16 – Apollo program: *Apollo 11* (Neil Armstrong, Buzz Aldrin, Michael Collins) lifts off toward the first landing on the Moon.
- July 18 – Chappaquiddick incident – Edward M. Kennedy drives off a bridge on his way home from a party on Chappaquiddick Island, Massachusetts. Mary Jo Kopechne, a former campaign aide to his brother, dies in the early morning hours of July 19 in the submerged car.
- July 19
  - John Fairfax lands in Hollywood Beach, Florida near Miami and becomes the first person to row across an

ocean solo, after 180 days spent at sea on board 25'
ocean rowboat 'Britannia' (left Gran Canaria on January
20, 1969).

- July 20 – Apollo program: The lunar module *Eagle*/Apollo 11
  lands on the lunar surface. An estimated 500 million people
  worldwide watch in awe as Neil Armstrong takes his
  historic first steps on the Moon at 10:56 pm ET (02:56 UTC
  July 21), the largest television audience for a live broadcast
  at that time.
- July 22 – Spanish dictator and head of state Francisco Franco
  appoints Prince Juan Carlos his successor.
- July 24
  - The *Apollo 11* astronauts return from the first successful
    Moon landing, and are placed in biological isolation for
    several days, on the chance they may have brought
    back lunar germs. The airless lunar environment is later
    determined to preclude microscopic life.
  - The Soviet Union returns Gerald Brooke to the United
    Kingdom in exchange for spies Peter and Helen Kroger
    (Morris and Lona Cohen).
- July 25 – Vietnam War: U.S. President Richard Nixon
  declares the Nixon Doctrine, stating that the United States
  now expects its Asian allies to take care of their own military
  defense. This starts the "Vietnamization" of the war.
- July 26 – The New York Chapter of the Young Lords is
  founded.
- July 30 – Vietnam War: U.S. President Richard Nixon makes
  an unscheduled visit to South Vietnam, meeting with
  President Nguyễn Văn Thiệu and U.S. military commanders.
- July 31 – The halfpenny ceases to be legal tender in the UK.

August

- August 4 – Vietnam War: At the apartment of French intermediary Jean Sainteny in Paris, U.S. representative Henry Kissinger and North Vietnamese representative Xuan Thuy begin secret peace negotiations. They eventually fail since both sides cannot agree to any terms.
- August 5 – Mariner program: *Mariner 7* makes its closest fly-by of Mars (3,524 kilometers) and proto-punk band The Stooges releases their homonym debut album.
- August 8
  - The Beatles at 11:30 have photographer Iain Macmillan take their photo on a zebra crossing on Abbey Road.
  - A fire breaks out in Bannerman's Castle in the Hudson River; most of the roof collapses and crashes down to the lower levels.
- August 9
  - The Haunted Mansion attraction opens at Disneyland California. Later versions open in Florida, Tokyo and Paris.
  - Followers of Charles Manson murder Sharon Tate, (who was 8 months pregnant), and her friends: Folgers coffee heiress Abigail Folger, Wojciech Frykowski, and Hollywood hairstylist Jay Sebring at the home of Tate and her husband, Roman Polanski, in Los Angeles. Also killed is Steven Parent, leaving from a visit to the Polanski's caretaker. More than 100 stab wounds are found on the victims, except for Parent, who had been shot almost as soon as the Manson Family entered the property.

- August 10 – The Manson Family kills Leno and Rosemary LaBianca, wealthy Los Angeles businessman and his wife.
- August 12 – Violence erupts after the Apprentice Boys of Derry march in Derry, Northern Ireland, resulting in a three-day communal riot known as the Battle of the Bogside.
- August 13 – Serious border clashes occur between the Soviet Union and the People's Republic of China.
- August 14 – British troops are deployed in Northern Ireland following the three-day Battle of the Bogside.
- August 15 – Captain D's is founded as "Mr. D's Seafood and Hamburgers" by Ray Danner with its first location opening in Donelson, Tennessee.
- August 15–August 18 – The Woodstock Festival is held in upstate New York, featuring some of the top rock musicians of the era.
- August 17 – Category 5 Hurricane Camille, the most powerful tropical cyclonic system at landfall in history, hits the Mississippi coast, killing 248 people and causing US$1.5 billion in damage (1969 dollars).
- August 20 – Florissant Fossil Beds National Monument is established in Florissant, CO, USA
- August 21
  - Donald and Doris Fisher open the first Gap store on Ocean Avenue in San Francisco.
  - Australian Denis Michael Rohan sets the Al-Aqsa Mosque on fire.
  - Strong violence on demonstration in Prague and Brno, Czechoslovakia. Military force contra citizens. Prague spring finally beaten.

September

- September 1 – A coup in Libya ousts King Idris, and brings Colonel Muammar Gaddafi to power.
- September 2
    - The first automatic teller machine in the United States is installed in Rockville Centre, New York.
    - Ho Chi Minh, former president of the Democratic Republic of Vietnam, dies.
- September 5 – Lieutenant William Calley is charged with 6 counts of premeditated murder, for the 1968 My Lai Massacre deaths of 109 Vietnamese civilians in My Lai, Vietnam.
- September 9 – Allegheny Airlines Flight 853 DC-9 collides in flight with a Piper PA-28, and crashes near Fairland, Indiana, killing all 83 persons in both aircraft.
- September 13 – The first-ever episode of *Scooby-Doo, Where Are You!* is broadcast on CBS: "What a Night for a Knight".
- September 20 – The very last theatrical Warner Bros. cartoon is released: the Merrie Melodies short *Injun Trouble*.
- September 22 – San Francisco Giant Willie Mays becomes the first player since Babe Ruth to hit 600 career home runs.
- September 22 – September 25 – An Islamic conference in Rabat, Morocco, following the al-Aqsa Mosque fire (August 21), condemns the Israeli claim of ownership of Jerusalem.
- September 23
    - China carries out an underground nuclear bomb test.
    - *Butch Cassidy and the Sundance Kid* (directed by George Roy Hill and starring Paul Newman and Robert Redford) opens to limited release in the U.S.

- September 24 – The *Chicago Eight* trial begins in Chicago, Illinois.
- September 25 – The Organisation of the Islamic Conference is founded.
- September 26
    - The Beatles release their *Abbey Road* album, receiving critical praise and enormous commercial success.
    - *The Brady Bunch* is broadcast for the first time on ABC.
- September 28 – The Social Democrats and the Free Democrats receive a majority of votes in the German parliamentary elections, and decide to form a common government.

October

- October 1
    - In Sweden, Olof Palme is elected Leader of the Social Democratic Worker`s Party, replacing Tage Erlander as Prime Minister on October 14.
    - The Beijing Subway begins operation.
- October 2 – A 1.2 megaton thermonuclear device is tested at Amchitka Island, Alaska. This test is code-named Project Milrow, the 11th test of the Operation Mandrel 1969–1970 underground nuclear test series. This test is known as a "calibration shot" to test if the island is fit for larger underground nuclear detonations.
- October 5
    - *Monty Python's Flying Circus* first airs on BBC One.
    - *Sazae-san* first airs on Fuji Television.

- October 9–October 12 – Days of Rage: In Chicago, the United States National Guard is called in to control demonstrations involving the radical Weathermen, in connection with the "Chicago Eight" Trial.
- October 11–October 16 – The New York Mets defeat the Baltimore Orioles four games to one in one of the greatest World Series upsets in baseball history.
- October 13
  - An unofficial strike amongst British mineworkers begins over the working hours of surface workers.
- October 15 – Vietnam War: Hundreds of thousands of people take part in Moratorium to End the War in Vietnam demonstrations across the United States.
- October 17
  - Willard S. Boyle and George Smith invent the CCD at Bell Laboratories (30 years later, this technology is widely used in digital cameras).
  - Fourteen black athletes are kicked off the University of Wyoming football team for wearing black armbands into their coach's office.
- October 21
  - Willy Brandt becomes Chancellor of West Germany.
  - General Siad Barre comes to power in Somalia in a coup, 6 days after the assassination of President Abdirashid Ali Shermarke.
- October 22 – Led Zeppelin release *Led Zeppelin II* to critical acclaim and commercial success.
- October 25 – Pink Floyd release their *Ummagumma* album.
- October 29 – The first message is sent over ARPANET, the forerunner of the internet.

- October 31
  - Wal-Mart incorporates as **Wal-Mart Stores, Inc.**
  - The disappearance of Patricia Spencer and Pamela Hobley occurs.

November

- November 3
  - Vietnam War: U.S. President Richard Nixon addresses the nation on television and radio, asking the "silent majority" to join him in solidarity with the Vietnam War effort, and to support his policies. Vice President Spiro Agnew denounces the President's critics as 'an effete corps of impudent snobs' and 'nattering nabobs of negativism'.
  - Süleyman Demirel of AP forms the new government of Turkey (31st government).
- November 9 – A group of American Indians, led by Richard Oakes, seizes Alcatraz Island for 19 months, inspiring a wave of renewed Indian pride and government reform.
- November 10 – *Sesame Street* is broadcast for the first time, on the National Educational Television (NET) network.
- November 12 – Vietnam War – My Lai Massacre: Independent investigative journalist Seymour Hersh breaks the My Lai story.
- November 14
  - Apollo program: NASA launches *Apollo 12* (Pete Conrad, Richard Gordon, Alan Bean), the second manned mission to the Moon.

- The SS United States the last active United States Lines passenger ship is withdrawn from service.
- November 15
  - Cold War: The Soviet submarine K-19 collides with the American submarine USS *Gato* in the Barents Sea.
  - Vietnam War: In Washington, D.C., 250,000–500,000 protesters stage a peaceful demonstration against the war, including a symbolic "March Against Death".
  - Regular colour television broadcasts begin on BBC1 and ITV in the United Kingdom.
  - Dave Thomas opens his first restaurant in a former steakhouse in downtown Columbus, Ohio. He names the chain *Wendy's* after his 8-year-old daughter, Melinda Lou (nicknamed "Wendy" by her siblings).
- November 17 – Cold War: Negotiators from the Soviet Union and the United States meet in Helsinki, to begin the SALT I negotiations aimed at limiting the number of strategic weapons on both sides.
- November 19
  - Apollo program: *Apollo 12* astronauts Charles Conrad and Alan Bean land at Oceanus Procellarum ("Ocean of Storms"), becoming the third and fourth humans to walk on the Moon.
  - Soccer great Pelé scores his 1,000th goal.
- November 20
  - Vietnam War: *The Plain Dealer* publishes explicit photographs of dead villagers from the My Lai Massacre in Vietnam.
  - Richard Oakes returns with 90 followers and offers to buy Alcatraz for $24 (he leaves the island January 1970).

- November 21
  - U.S. President Richard Nixon and Japanese Premier Eisaku Satō agree in Washington, D.C. to the return of Okinawa to Japanese control in 1972. Under the terms of the agreement, the U.S. retains rights to military bases on the island, but they must be nuclear-free.
  - The first ARPANET link is established (the progenitor of the global Internet).
  - The United States Senate votes down the Supreme Court nomination of Clement Haynsworth, the first such rejection since 1930.
- November 24 – Apollo program: The *Apollo 12* spacecraft splashes down safely in the Pacific Ocean, ending the second manned mission to the Moon.
- November 25 – John Lennon returns his MBE medal to protest the British government's involvement in the Nigerian Civil War.

December

- December 1 – Vietnam War: The first draft lottery in the United States is held since World War II (on January 4, 1970, *The New York Times* will run a long article, "Statisticians Charge Draft Lottery Was Not Random").
- December 2 – The Boeing 747 jumbo jet makes its first passenger flight. It carries 191 people, most of them reporters and photographers, from Seattle, to New York City.

- December 4 – Black Panther Party members Fred Hampton and Mark Clark are shot dead in their sleep during a raid by 14 Chicago police officers.
- December 5 – The Rolling Stones release Let it Bleed.
- December 6 – The Altamont Free Concert is held at the Altamont Speedway in northern California. Hosted by The Rolling Stones, it is an attempt at a "Woodstock West" and is best known for the uproar of violence that occurred. It is viewed by many as the "end of the sixties."
- December 12 – The Piazza Fontana bombing in Italy (Strage di Piazza Fontana) takes place.
- December 14 – The murder of Diane Maxwell takes place, when the 25-year-old phone operator is found sexually assaulted and killed (the case remains unsolved until 2003).
- December 24
  - Charles Manson is allowed to defend himself at the Tate-LaBianca murder trial.
  - The oil company Phillips Petroleum made the first oil discovery in the Norwegian sector of North Sea.
  - Nigerian troops capture Umuahia, the last Biafran capital before its dissolution became Owerri
- December 27 – The Liberal Democratic Party wins 47.6% of the votes in the Japanese general election, 1969. Future prime ministers Yoshirō Mori and Tsutomu Hata and future kingmaker Ichirō Ozawa are elected for the first time.
- December 28 – The Young Lords take over the First Spanish Methodist Church in East Harlem.
- December 30 – The Linwood bank robbery leaves two police officers dead.

Date unknown

- Common African, Malagasy and Mauritian Organization (OCAMM) (Organisation Commune Africaine Malgache et Mauricienne).
- Reported as being the year the first strain of the AIDS virus (HIV) migrates to the United States via Haiti.
- Summer sees the invention of Unix under the potential name "Unics" (after Multics).
- Women are allowed membership in the Future Farmers of America (now the National FFA Organization).
- Long John Silver's restaurant chain opens its first store in Lexington, Kentucky.
- Arthur Treacher's Fish and Chips is founded by S. Robert Davis and Dave Thomas and its first location in Columbus, Ohio opens for business.
- The Montreal Expos debut as Major League Baseball's first team outside the United States.

Births

January

Michael Schumacher

Jason Bateman

Dave Grohl

Tiësto

Dave Bautista

Patton Oswalt

- January 2
  - Dean Francis Alfar, Filipino author
  - Tommy Morrison, American boxer (d. 2013)
  - Christy Turlington, American fashion model
  - Robby Gordon, American race car driver
- January 3 – Michael Schumacher, German race car driver

- January 5 – Marilyn Manson, American rock musician
- January 6 – Norman Reedus, American actor
- January 8 – Jeff Abercrombie, American rock musician (Fuel)
- January 11 – Kyōko Hikami, Japanese voice actress
- January 13 – Stephen Hendry, British snooker player
- January 14
  - Jason Bateman, American actor, director and producer
  - David Grohl, American rock drummer and composer (Nirvana, Foo Fighters)
- January 15 – Meret Becker, German actress and musician
- January 16
  - Roy Jones Jr., American boxer
  - Per "Dead" Ohlin, Norwegian vocalist (d. 1991)
- January 17
  - Lukas Moodysson, Swedish film director
  - Tiësto, Dutch trance DJ
- January 18 – Dave Bautista, American actor, professional mixed martial artist and professional wrestler
- January 19 – Junior Seau, American NFL player (d. 2012)
- January 20 – Patrick K. Kroupa, American writer, hacker
- January 27
  - Cornelius, Japanese rock musician, singer and producer (Flipper's Guitar)
  - Patton Oswalt, American stand-up comedian, writer, actor and voice actor
- January 28 – Kathryn Morris, American actress
- January 29 – Hyde, Japanese rock musician, singer and guitarist

February

Jennifer Aniston

Birdman

Patrick Monahan

- February 1
  - Andrew Breitbart, American writer and publisher (d. 2012)
  - Gabriel Batistuta, Argentine footballer
- February 3

- Retief Goosen, South African golfer
- Beau Biden, 44th Attorney General of Delaware (d. 2015)
- February 5 – Bobby Brown, African-American singer
- February 9 – Ian Eagle, American sports announcer
- February 10 – Laura Dern, American actress
- February 11
  - Jennifer Aniston, American actress, director, producer and businesswoman
  - Bill Warner, American motorcycle racer (d. 2013)
- February 12
  - Darren Aronofsky, American film director
  - Hong Myung-bo, South Korean footballer
  - Brad Werenka, Canadian ice-hockey player
- February 13
  - Ahlam, Arabic singer
  - J. B. Blanc, French voice actor
- February 15 – Birdman, American rapper, entertainer, and record producer
- February 19 – Burton C. Bell, American rock vocalist/lyricist
- February 20 – Keiji Takayama, Japanese professional wrestler
- February 21
  - Bosson, Swedish singer-songwriter
  - Petra Kronberger, Austrian alpine skier
- February 22 – Thomas Jane, American actor
- February 23
  - Michael Campbell, New Zealand golfer
  - Marc Wauters, Belgian cyclist
- February 24 – Christine Ng, Hong Kong actress

- February 28
    - Robert Sean Leonard, American actor
    - Patrick Monahan, American musician and singer

March

Javier Bardem

Terrence Howard

Ali Daei

- March 1
    - Javier Bardem, Spanish actor
    - Dafydd Ieuan, Welsh rock drummer
    - Litefoot, Native American actor
- March 4

- o Chaz Bono, American LGBT rights activist
- o Annie Shizuka Inoh, Taiwanese actress
- o Patrick Roach, Canadian actor
- March 7 – Todd Williams, American long-distance runner
- March 10 – Paget Brewster, American actress
- March 11
  - o Soraya, Colombian singer and multi-instrumentalist (d. 2006)
  - o Terrence Howard, American actor and singer
- March 12
  - o Graham Coxon, English singer-songwriter, multi-instrumentalist (Blur) and painter
  - o Akemi Okamura, Japanese voice actress
- March 13 – Susanna Mälkki, Finnish conductor
- March 15
  - o Timo Kotipelto, Finnish musician
  - o Yutaka Take, Japanese jockey
  - o Kim Raver, American actress
- March 16 – Markus Lanz, German-Italian television presenter
- March 17 – Alexander McQueen, British fashion designer (d. 2010)
- March 18 – Vassily Ivanchuk, Ukrainian chess grandmaster
- March 19
  - o Patrick Tam, Hong Kong actor
  - o Connor Trinneer, American actor
- March 20 – Kenneth Keith Kallenbach, American comedian (d. 2008)
- March 21
  - o Ali Daei, Iranian football player

- ○ Jaya, Filipino pop singer
- March 24 – Stephan Eberharter, Austrian alpine skier
- March 25 – Jeffrey Walker, English musician
- March 27 – Pauley Perrette, American actress
- March 28
    - ○ Rodney Atkins, America country music singer-songwriter
    - ○ Laurie Brett, Scottish actress
- March 29 – Chiaki Ishikawa, Japanese singer (See-Saw)
- March 31 – Samantha Brown, American television host

April

Renée Zellweger

Paul Rudd

- April 1 – Fadl Shaker, Lebanese singer
- April 2 – Ajay Devgn, Bollywood actor
- April 3 – Lance Storm, Canadian professional wrestler
- April 6
  - Bret Boone, American baseball player
  - Paul Rudd, American actor, comedian, writer and producer
- April 9 – Debbie Schlussel, political commentator and film critic
- April 10 – Billy Jayne, American actor
- April 11
  - Cerys Matthews, Welsh singer
  - Caren Miosga, German journalist and television presenter
  - Chisato Moritaka, Japanese singer
- April 12 – Michael Jackson, former NFL wide receiver
- April 17 – Henry Ian Cusick, Peruvian actor
- April 19
  - Shannon Lee, Chinese-American actress

- Susan Polgar, Hungarian chess player
- April 20 – Marietta Slomka, German journalist
- April 21 – Toby Stephens, English actor
- April 22 – Dion Dublin, English footballer
- April 25
  - Vanessa Beecroft, Italian artist
  - Joe Buck, American sports announcer
  - Renée Zellweger, American actress and producer

May

Wes Anderson

Cate Blanchett

David Boreanaz

- May 1 – Wes Anderson, American director, producer, screenwriter and actor
- May 2 – Brian Lara, West Indian cricketer
- May 3 – Daryl F. Mallett, American author and actor
- May 4
  - Micah Aivazoff, Canadian ice hockey player
  - Christina Billotte, American musician
- May 5 – Hideki Irabu, Japanese baseball player (d. 2011)
- May 6 – Jim Magilton, Northern Irish footballer
- May 7 – Eagle Eye Cherry, Swedish-born musician
- May 9 – Amber, Dutch musician
- May 10 – Dennis Bergkamp, Dutch soccer player
- May 12 – Kevin Nalty, American YouTube comedian
- May 13
  - Nikos Aliagas, French-born television host
  - Brian Carroll (a.k.a. Buckethead), American guitarist
- May 14
  - Cate Blanchett, Australian actress
  - Danny Wood, American singer (New Kids on the Block)

- May 15
  - Asalah Nasri, Syrian singer
  - Emmitt Smith, American football player
- May 16
  - David Boreanaz, American actor
  - Tracey Gold, American actress
  - Steve Lewis, American athlete
- May 18 – Martika, American singer
- May 21 – Georgiy R. Gongadze, Ukrainian journalist (d. 2000)
- May 25
  - Anne Heche, American actress
  - Stacy London, American fashion consultant and media personality
- May 26
  - Siri Lindley, American triathlete
  - Musetta Vander, South African actress
- May 28 – Rob Ford, Canadian politician (d. 2016)

June

Peter Dinklage

Steffi Graf

Ice Cube

Oliver Kahn

Achinoam Nini

- June 4
  - Eugene Chung, Korean-American football player
  - Rob Huebel, American comedian
  - Takako Minekawa, Japanese musician, composer and writer
- June 7
  - Alina Astafei, Romanian-German high jumper
  - Prince Joachim of Denmark
  - Kim Rhodes, American actress
- June 8 – J. P. Manoux, American actor
- June 11
  - Peter Dinklage, American actor
  - Steven Drozd, American rock drummer (The Flaming Lips)
- June 12 – Zsolt Daczi, Hungarian rock guitarist (d. 2007)
- June 13 – Søren Rasted, Danish musician (Aqua)
- June 14
  - Steffi Graf, German tennis player
  - MC Ren, American rapper (N.W.A)
- June 15
  - Ice Cube, African-American rapper and actor

- Jansher Khan, Pakistani squash player
- Oliver Kahn, German football goalkeeper
- Maurice Odumbe, Kenyan cricketer
- June 17 – Paul Tergat, Kenyan athlete
- June 18
  - Haki Doku, Albanian para-cyclist
  - Pål Pot Pamparius, Norwegian rock guitarist and keyboardist (Turbonegro)
- June 19 – Trine Pallesen, Danish actress
- June 20 – Paulo Bento, Portuguese football player and coach
- June 23
  - Fernanda Ribeiro, Portuguese long-distance runner
  - Achinoam Nini (Noa), Israeli singer
- June 24
  - Rich Eisen, American television journalist
  - Sissel Kyrkjebø, Norwegian singer
- June 25
  - Matt Gallant, American television host
  - Storm Large, American singer and actor
  - Zim Zum, American guitarist
- June 29
  - Toru Hashimoto, Japanese local governor
  - Ilan Mitchell-Smith, American actor
- June 30 – Sanath Jayasuriya, Sri Lankan cricketer

July

Ken Jeong

Jennifer Lopez

Triple H

Simon Baker

- July 3 – Gedeon Burkhard, German actor
- July 4 – Jordan Sonnenblick, American teacher and novelist
- July 5 – John LeClair, American hockey player
- July 7
  - Sylke Otto, German luger
  - Joe Sakic, Canadian hockey player
- July 8 – Sugizo, Japanese guitarist and singer
- July 10
  - Gale Harold, American actor
  - Jonas Kaufmann, German operatic tenor
- July 11 – David Tao, Taiwanese singer-songwriter
- July 13 – Ken Jeong, American actor, comedian and physician
- July 16 – Sahra Wagenknecht, German politician
- July 18 – Masanori Murakawa, Japanese wrestler
- July 20 – Josh Holloway, American actor
- July 21
  - Godfrey, American comedian and actor
  - Isabell Werth, German equestrian
- July 22 – Despina Vandi, Greek singer

- July 24 – Jennifer Lopez, American actress and singer
- July 26 – Tanni Grey-Thompson, born Carys Grey, British Paralympian
- July 27
  - Pavel Hapal, Czech footballer
  - Triple H (aka Paul Levesque), American wrestler
- July 28
  - Michael Amott, English musician
  - Tichina Arnold, African-American actress (*Everybody Hates Chris*)
- July 29 – Timothy Omundson, American actor
- July 30
  - Simon Baker, Australian actor and director
  - Mandakini (aka Yasmeen Joseph), Indian Bollywood actress
- July 31 – Antonio Conte, Italian football player and manager

August

Edward Norton

Christian Slater

Matthew Perry

Jack Black

- August 2
  - Jan Axel Blomberg, Norwegian drummer
  - Fernando Couto, Portuguese footballer
- August 4 – Max Cavalera, Brazilian musician and singer (Soulfly)

- August 5 – Graham Elwood, American comedian and game show host
- August 6 – Elliott Smith, American musician (d. 2003)
- August 8
  - Dick Togo, Japanese professional wrestler
  - Faye Wong, Hong Kong singer and actress
- August 9 – Troy Percival, American baseball player
- August 10 – Brian Drummond, Canadian voice actor
- August 11
  - Ashley Jensen, British actress
  - Vanderlei de Lima, Brazilian long-distance runner
- August 12 – Tanita Tikaram, German-born British singer-songwriter
- August 13 – Midori Ito, Japanese figure skater
- August 15
  - Justin Broadrick, British musician
  - Kevin Cheng, Hong Kong television actor and singer
- August 17 – Donnie Wahlberg, American singer (New Kids on the Block)
- August 18
  - Everlast, American singer, rapper, and songwriter
  - Edward Norton, American actor
  - Christian Slater, American actor
- August 19
  - Nate Dogg, African-American rapper (d. 2011)
  - Matthew Perry, Canadian-American actor
  - Clay Walker, American singer
- August 21 – Oliver Geissen, German television presenter
- August 28 – Jack Black, American actor and musician
- August 29

- Lucero, Mexican singer and actress
- Joe Swail, Northern Irish snooker player

September

Catherine Zeta-Jones

Erika Eleniak

- September 2
  - Cedric "K-Ci" Hailey, American singer, one half of R&B duo K-Ci & JoJo
  - Dave Naz, American photographer
- September 3 – Robert Karlsson, Swedish golfer
- September 5 – Dweezil Zappa, American actor and musician
- September 7
  - Jean-Benoît Dunckel, French musician (Air)
  - Diane Farr, American actress
  - Jimmy Urine, American singer

- September 8 – Gary Speed, Welsh footballer and manager (d. 2011)
- September 9 – Rachel Hunter, New Zealand model and actress
- September 10 – Ai Jing, Chinese singer
- September 11 – Crystal Lewis, American Christian musician
- September 12
  - Ángel Cabrera, Argentine golfer
  - Shigeki Maruyama, Japanese golfer
- September 13 – Shane Warne, Australian cricketer
- September 14 – Bong Joon-ho, South Korean screenwriter and film director
- Kerry Butters - Author
- September 17 – Ken Doherty, Irish snooker player
- September 19 – Michael Symon, American chef and television personality
- September 23 – Mahir Çağrı, Turkish Internet celebrity
- September 24
  - Shawn "Clown" Crahan, American rock percussionist
  - DeVante Swing, American music producer
- September 25
  - Yves Amyot, Québécois actor
  - Hansie Cronje, South African cricketer (d. 2002)
  - Hal Sparks, American actor and comedian
  - Heather Stewart-Whyte, British model
  - Catherine Zeta-Jones, Welsh actress
  - Bill Simmons, American sports columnist
- September 26
  - Victor N'Gembo-Mouanda, Congolese author
  - Paul Warhurst, English football player

- September 29 – Erika Eleniak, American model and actress

October

Zach Galifianakis

Gwen Stefani

Julia Ann

Wyclef Jean

Trey Parker

- October 1
  - Zach Galifianakis, American actor and stand-up comedian
  - Igor Ulanov, Russian hockey player
- October 2
  - Jun Akiyama, Japanese professional wrestler
  - Mitch English, American actor and television host
- October 3
  - Gwen Stefani, American singer and television host
  - Tetsuya, Japanese musician
- October 5 – Elizabeth Azcona Bocock, Honduran politician
- October 6 – Ogün Temizkanoğlu, Turkish football player
- October 7
  - Benny Chan Ho Man, Hong Kong actor

- o Benny Chan Muk-Sing, Hong Kong film director
- October 8 – Julia Ann, American porn actress
- October 9
    - o PJ Harvey, British singer-songwriter
    - o Steve McQueen, English film director, producer and screenwriter
- October 10 – Brett Favre, American football player
- October 12 – Judit Mascó, Spanish model, television host and writer
- October 13
    - o Rhett Akins, American country singer
    - o Nancy Kerrigan, American figure skater
    - o Cady McClain, American actress and director
- October 14
    - o Kosuke Okano, Japanese voice actor
    - o David Strickland, American actor (d. 1999)
- October 17
    - o Ernie Els, South African golfer
    - o Jesús Ángel García, Spanish race walker
    - o Wood Harris, American actor
    - o Wyclef Jean, Haitian rapper
    - o Nancy Sullivan, American actress
- October 19, Trey Parker, American voice actor, comedian, screenwriter, composer, director and producer
- October 20
    - o Laurie Daley, Australian rugby league player
    - o Juan González, American baseball player
- October 21
    - o Michael Hancock, Australian rugby league footballer
    - o Angela Vincent, Australian actress

- October 24
  - Peter Dolving, Swedish musician
  - Adela Noriega, Mexican actress
- October 25
  - Josef Beránek, Czech ice hockey player
  - Oleg Salenko, Russian football player
  - Alex Webster, American bassist
  - Grant Gipson, Arctic Warfare Specialist
- October 29 – Ha Hee-ra, Korean actress
- October 30
  - Snow, Canadian singer
  - Stanislav Gross, Prime Minister of the Czech Republic (d. 2015)
- October 31 – Kim Rossi Stuart, Italian actor and director

November

Sean Combs

Matthew McConaughey

Tomas N'evergreen

- November 1 – Diane Parish, English actress
- November 2 – Reginald Arvizu (aka Fieldy Snuts), American bassist
- November 3 – Robert Miles, Swiss-Italian record producer and DJ
- November 4
  - Sean Combs, African-American rapper (aka Puff Daddy, P. Diddy)
  - Matthew McConaughey, American actor
- November 7
  - Michelle Clunie, American actress
  - Hélène Grimaud, French pianist

- Bryant H. McGill, American poet
- November 8 – Roxana Zal, American actress
- November 9
    - Sandra Denton, African-American rapper (Salt-n-Pepa)
    - Allison Wolfe, American musician
- November 10
    - Faustino Asprilla, Colombian football player
    - Jens Lehmann, German football player
    - Ellen Pompeo, American actress
- November 11 – Carson Kressley, American fashion expert
- November 12
    - Johnny Gosch, American child kidnap victim
    - Tomas N'evergreen, Danish singer
    - Heinz-Christian Strache, Austrian politician
- November 13
    - Gerard Butler, Scottish actor
    - Josh Mancell, American freelance composer and multi-instrumentalist
- November 17
    - Jean-Michel Saive, Belgian table tennis player
    - Ryotaro Okiayu, Japanese voice actor
- November 18
    - Kathleen van Brempt, Belgian politician
    - Sam Cassell, American basketball player
    - Ahmed Helmy, Egyptian actor
- November 19 – Ertuğrul Sağlam, Turkish football coach and former player
- November 20 – Sakura, Japanese musician
- November 21 – Ken Griffey, Jr., American baseball player
- November 23 – Robin Padilla, Filipino actor

- November 24 – David Adeang, Nauruan politician
- November 28 – Lexington Steele, American actor and film director
- November 29
  - Chris Baker, American race car driver
  - Pierre van Hooijdonk, Dutch footballer
  - Kasey Keller, American Major League Soccer player
  - Mariano Rivera, Panamanian Major League Baseball player

December

Jay-Z

Viswanathan Anand

Ed Miliband

- December 3 – Bill Steer, English musician
- December 4 – Jay-Z, African-American rapper
- December 5 – Alex Kapp Horner, American actress
- December 7 – Suhail A. Khan, American activist
- December 8 – Kerry Earnhardt, American race car driver
- December 9 – Jakob Dylan, American singer-songwriter (The Wallflowers)
- December 11
  - Viswanathan Anand, Indian chess Grandmaster
  - Sean Grande, American basketball announcer
- December 13 – Hideo Ishikawa, Japanese voice actor
- December 14 – Archie Kao, Chinese-American film and television actor
- December 15 – Rick Law, American illustrator and producer
- December 16 – Michelle Smith, Irish swimmer
- December 17 – Chuck Liddell, American mixed martial arts fighter
- December 18
  - Irvin Duguid, Scottish rock keyboard player (Stiltskin)
  - Mille Petrozza, German-Italian rock vocalist and guitarist (Kreator)

- o Joe Randa, American Major League Baseball player and radio talk-show host
- December 19
  - o Richard Hammond, British TV presenter
  - o Lauren Sánchez, American news anchor
  - o Kristy Swanson, American actress
  - o Villano IV, Mexican wrestler
- December 20 – Chisa Yokoyama, Japanese voice actress
- December 21
  - o Julie Delpy, French actress
  - o Magnus Samuelsson, Swedish bodybuilder and former World's Strongest Man
- December 23
  - o Greg Biffle, American race car driver
  - o Martha Byrne, American actress and singer
  - o Rob Pelinka, American sports agent
- December 24
  - o Brad Anderson, American wrestler
  - o Milan Blagojevic, Australian soccer player
  - o Pernille Fischer Christensen, Danish film director
  - o Taro Goto, Japanese soccer player
  - o Stephen Shaun Griffiths, English serial killer
  - o Leavander Johnson, American lightweight boxer (d. 2005)
  - o Ryuji Kato, Japanese soccer player
  - o Nick Love, English film director and writer
  - o Miyuki Matsushita, Japanese voice actress
  - o Clinton McKinnon, American musician
  - o Sean Cameron Michael, South African actor and singer

- Ed Miliband, English academic and politician, Minister for the Cabinet Office
- Mark Millar, Scottish author
- Luis Musrri, Chilean soccer player
- Mariko Shiga, Japanese voice actress (d. 1989)
- Oleg Skripochka, Russian cosmonaut
- Gintaras Staučė, Lithuanian soccer player
- Chen Yueling, American race walker
- Jonathan Zittrain, American professor
- Michael Zucchet, American economist and politician, Mayor of San Diego
- December 25 – Nicolas Godin, French musician (Air)
- December 28 – Linus Torvalds, Finnish computer programmer
- December 29 – George Fisher, (aka "CorpseGrinder"), American musician
- December 30 – Jason Kay, English singer (Jamiroquai)
- December 31 – Dominik Diamond, Scottish presenter and newspaper columnist

Date unknown

- Molly Kiely, American cartoonist

Deaths

January

- Daisy and Violet Hilton, English conjoined twin actresses (b. 1908; bodies discovered on January 4, 1969)
- January 1 – Barton MacLane, American actor (b. 1902)
- January 2 – Gilbert Miller(*aka Gilbert Heron*) American theatrical producer (b. 1884)
- January 3 – Howard McNear, American actor (b. 1905)
- January 4 – William M. Zachacki, Americam politician (b. 1913)
- January 8 – Albert Hill, British athlete (b. 1889)
- January 16 – Vernon Duke, Russian-American songwriter (b. 1903)
- January 19 – Jan Palach, Czech student protester (suicide) (b. 1948)
- January 25 – Irene Castle, English dancer (b. 1893)
- January 27 – Charles Winninger, American actor (b. 1884)
- January 29 – Allen Dulles, American director of the Central Intelligence Agency (b. 1893)
- January 30 – Georges Pire, Belgian monk, recipient of the Nobel Peace Prize (b. 1910)
- January 31 – Meher Baba, Indian spiritual master (b. 1894)

February

Boris Karloff

Levi Eshkol

- February 2 – Boris Karloff, English actor (b. 1887)
- February 3 – Eduardo Mondlane, Mozambican FRELIMO leader (assassinated) (b. 1920)
- February 5 – Conrad Hilton, Jr., American heir and socialite (b. 1926)
- February 9 – George "Gabby" Hayes, American actor (b. 1885)
- February 12 – Paltiel Daykan, Russian-born Israeli jurist (b. 1885)

- February 13 – Florence Mary Taylor, Australia's first female architect (b. 1879)
- February 14 – Thelma Ritter, American actress (b. 1902)
- February 15 – Pee Wee Russell, American jazz musician (b. 1906)
- February 20 – Ernest Ansermet, Swiss conductor (b. 1883)
- February 23 – King Saud of Saudi Arabia (b. 1902)
- February 26
  - Levi Eshkol, Prime Minister of Israel (b. 1895)
  - Karl Jaspers, German psychiatrist and philosopher (b. 1883)
- February 27 – John Boles, American actor (b. 1895)

March

Dwight D. Eisenhower

- March 4 – Nicholas Schenck, Russian-born film empresario (b. 1881)
- March 9 – Charles Brackett, American novelist and screenwriter (b. 1892)
- March 11
  - Daniel E. Barbey, American admiral (b. 1889)
  - John Wyndham, British author (b. 1903)

- March 14 – Ben Shahn, Lithuanian-born American artist (b. 1898)
- March 18 – Barbara Bates, American actress (b. 1925)
- March 20 – Henri Longchambon, French politician (b. 1896)
- March 21 – Pinky Higgins, American baseball player and manager (b. 1909)
- March 25
  - Billy Cotton, British entertainer and bandleader (b. 1899)
  - Max Eastman, American writer (b. 1883)
  - Alan Mowbray, English actor (b. 1896)
- March 26
  - John Kennedy Toole, American author (b. 1937)
  - B. Traven, German writer
- March 28 – Dwight D. Eisenhower, 34th President of the United States (b. 1890)

April

- April 5 – Shelby Storck, American television producer (b. 1917)
- April 6 – Gabriel Chevallier, French writer (b. 1895)
- April 7 – Rómulo Gallegos, Venezuelan president and writer (b. 1884)
- April 15 – Ain-Ervin Mere, Estonian Nazi war criminal (b. 1903)
- April 26 – Morihei Ueshiba, Japanese martial artist and founder of aikido (b. 1883)

May

Jeffrey Hunter

- May 1 – Ella Logan, American actress (b. 1913)
- May 2 – Franz von Papen, Chancellor of Germany (b. 1879)
- May 3
    - Karl Freund, German cinematographer (b. 1890)
    - Amy Ashwood Garvey, Jamaican pan-African activist (b. 1897)
    - Zakir Hussain; Indian politician, 3rd President of India (b. 1897)
- May 4 – Osbert Sitwell, English writer (b. 1892)
- May 14
    - Enid Bennett, American actress (b. 1893)
    - Frederick Lane, Australian swimmer (b. 1888)
- May 15 – Robert R., American HIV/AIDS victim (b. 1953)
- May 19 – Coleman Hawkins, American musician (b. 1904)
- May 20 – Fred Sherman, American actor (b. 1905)
- May 23 – Jimmy McHugh, American composer (b. 1894)
- May 24 – Mitzi Green, American actress (b. 1920)
- May 27 – Jeffrey Hunter, American actor (b. 1926)
- May 28 – Rhys Williams, Welsh actor (b. 1897)

June

Judy Garland

- June 1 – Ivar Ballangrud, Norwegian Olympic speed skater (b. 1904)
- June 2 – Leo Gorcey, American actor (b. 1917)
- June 4 – Rafael Osuna, Mexican tennis champion (b. 1938)
- June 5 – Miles Dempsey, British general (b. 1896)
- June 8 – Robert Taylor, American actor (b. 1911)
- June 13 – Martita Hunt, British actress (b. 1899)
- June 16 – Harold Alexander, 1st Earl Alexander of Tunis, British field marshal (b. 1891)
- June 19 – Natalie Talmadge, American actress (b. 1898)
- June 21 – Maureen Connolly, American tennis player (b. 1934)
- June 22 – Judy Garland, American actress and singer (b. 1922)
- June 24 – Willy Ley, German science writer and space advocate (b. 1906)
- June 29 – Moise Tshombe, Congolese politician (b. 1919)

July

Brian Jones

Walter Gropius

- July 2
  - Mikio Naruse, Japanese film director (b. 1905)
  - Michael DiBiase, American wrestler (b 1923)
- July 3 – Brian Jones, British rock musician (The Rolling Stones) (b. 1942)
- July 5
  - Ben Alexander, American actor (b. 1911)
  - Walter Gropius, German architect (b. 1883)
  - Tom Mboya, Kenyan politician (assassinated) (b. 1930)

- ○ Lambert Hillyer, American film director (b. 1889)
  - ○ Leo McCarey, American film director (b. 1898)
- July 7 – Gladys Swarthout, American opera singer (b. 1900)
- July 9 – Raizō Tanaka, Japanese admiral (b. 1892)
- July 15 – Peter van Eyck, German-American actor (b. 1911)
- July 18
  - ○ Mary Jo Kopechne, American teacher, secretary, and political campaign specialist (b. 1940)
  - ○ Barbara Pepper, American actress (b. 1915)
- July 20
  - ○ Bertram "Bert" Cooper, American advertising executive (b. 1886)
  - ○ Cathy Wayne, pop entertainer, first Australian woman killed in Vietnam War (b. 1949)
- July 24 – Witold Gombrowicz, Polish novelist and dramatist (b. 1904)
- July 25 – Otto Dix, German painter (b. 1891)
- July 26
  - ○ Frank Loesser, American songwriter (b. 1910)
  - ○ Raymond Walburn, American actor (b. 1887)
- July 28 – Ramón Grau, Cuban president (b. 1882)

August

Theodor Adorno

Otto Stern

- August 6 – Theodor W. Adorno, German sociologist and philosopher (b. 1903)
- August 9
  - Abigail Folger, American socialite, Folgers Coffee heiress, and social worker (b. 1943)
  - Cecil Frank Powell, British physicist, Nobel Prize laureate (b. 1903)
  - Jay Sebring, American celebrity hair stylist (b. 1933)
  - Sharon Tate, American actress (b. 1943)
- August 14 – Leonard Woolf, English writer (b. 1880)
- August 17
  - Ludwig Mies van der Rohe, German-American architect (b. 1886)
  - Otto Stern, German physicist, Nobel Prize laureate (b. 1888)
- August 18 – Mildred Davis, American actress (b. 1901)
- August 20 – Dudley D. Watkins, Scottish illustrator for D. C. Thomson & Co. (b. 1907)
- August 25 – Harry Hammond Hess, American geologist and United States Navy officer in World War II (b. 1906)
- August 27
  - Dame Ivy Compton-Burnett, English novelist (b. 1884)

- ○ Erika Mann, German writer (b. 1905)
- August 31 – Rocky Marciano, American boxer (b. 1923)

September

Ho Chi Minh

- September 2 – Ho Chi Minh, President of Vietnam (b. 1890)
- September 3 – John Lester, American cricketer (b. 1871)
- September 6 – Arthur Friedenreich, Brazilian footballer (b. 1892)
- September 7 – Gavin Maxwell, Scottish naturalist and author (b. 1914)
- September 8 – Bud Collyer, American radio and television personality (b. 1908)
- September 12 – Terry de la Mesa Allen, Sr., American general (b. 1888)
- September 19 – Rex Ingram, American actor (b. 1895)

October

- October 4 – Natalino Otto, Italian singer (b. 1912)
- October 6 – Walter Hagen, American golf champion (b. 1892)
- October 7 – Ture Nerman, Swedish politician (b. 1886)

- October 8 – Eduardo Ciannelli, Italian actor and singer (b. 1889)
- October 11 – Kazimierz Sosnkowski, General of the Polish Army (b. 1885)
- October 12 – Sonja Henie, Norwegian figure skater (b. 1912)
- October 14
  - Arnie Herber, American football player (Green Bay Packers) and a member of the Pro Football Hall of Fame) (b. 1910)
  - August Sang, Estonian poet and literary translator (b. 1914)
- October 15
  - Rod La Rocque, American actor (b. 1896)
  - Abdirashid Ali Shermarke, President of Somalia (assassinated) (b. 1919)
- October 21
  - Jack Kerouac, American author (b. 1922)
  - Wacław Sierpiński, Polish mathematician (b. 1882)
- October 30 – Pops Foster, American musician (b. 1892)

November

- November 5 – Lloyd Corrigan, American actor (b. 1900)
- November 8 – Vesto Slipher, American astronomer (b. 1875)
- November 11 – Frank Mills (politician), American politician in Ohio legislature (1904)
- November 12 – William F. Friedman, American cryptanalyst (b. 1891)
- November 15
  - Roy D'Arcy, American actor (b. 1894)

- o Ignacio Aldecoa, Spanish writer (b. 1925)
- o Iskander Mirza, first President of Pakistan (b. 1899)
- o Billy Southworth, American baseball manager (St. Louis Cardinals) and a member of the MLB Hall of Fame (b. 1893)
- November 18 – Joseph P. Kennedy, Sr., American politician (b. 1888)
- November 28 – Roy Barcroft, American actor (b. 1902)

December

Claude Dornier

- December 2 – José María Arguedas, Peruvian novelist, poet, and anthropologist (b. 1911).
- December 3 – Ruth White, American actress (b. 1914)
- December 4
  - o Mark Clark, American Black Panther (b. 1947)
  - o Fred Hampton, American Black Panther (b. 1948)
  - o Hugh Oswald Short, aviation pioneer; CEO, Short Brothers (b. 1883)
- December 5
  - o Princess Alice of Battenberg (b. 1885)
  - o Claude Dornier, German airplane builder (b. 1884)

- December 7 – Eric Portman, English actor (b. 1901)
- December 12 – Magic Sam, American musician (b. 1937)
- December 13
  - Raymond A. Spruance, American admiral and ambassador (b. 1886)
  - Spencer Williams, American actor (b. 1893)
- December 17 – Artur da Costa e Silva, Brazilian marshal and statesman, 27th President of Brazil (b. 1899)
- December 21 – Georges Catroux, French Army general and colonial governor (b. 1877)
- December 22
  - Josef von Sternberg, Austrian film director (b. 1894)
  - Enrique Peñaranda, 45th President of Bolivia (b. 1892)
- December 24
  - Stanisław Błeszyński, Polish entomologist (b. 1927)
  - Cortelia Clark, African American blues singer and guitarist (b. 1907)
  - Olivia FitzRoy, British author of children's books (b. 1921)
  - Seabury Quinn, American author (b. 1889)
  - Alfred B. Skar, Norwegian politician (b. 1896)
- December 29 – Ricardo de la Guardia, former President of Panama (b. 1899)
- December 31 – Joseph Yablonski, murdered American labor leader (b. 1910)

Date unknown

- George de la Warr, British alternative physician (b. 1904)

Nobel Prizes

- Physics – Murray Gell-Mann
- Chemistry – Derek Harold Richard Barton, Odd Hassel
- Medicine – Max Delbrück, Alfred Hershey, Salvador Luria
- Literature – Samuel Beckett
- Peace – International Labour Organization
- Economics – Ragnar Frisch, Jan Tinbergen

In the News.

Dwight D. Eisenhower dies.

Thousands of party-goers sludge through the mud to experience four days of rock n' roll at a place called Woodstock.

Charles Manson and other members of his cult murder actress Sharon Tate and six others.

First commerical 747 goes into service.

On January 29th, The Beatles perform in public for the final time as a group.

Easy Rider (starring Peter Fonda) is the forerunner of a new wave of youth-oriented movies.

The most popular series on TV include *Rowan & Martin's Laugh-In*, *Gunsmoke*, **and** *Bonanza*.

Apollo 11 lands the first man on the moon in 1969.

Richard M. Nixon is inaugurated 37th President of the US (Jan. 20).

Movies - **Midnight Cowboy, Butch Cassidy and the Sundance Kid, The Wild Bunch, Easy Rider, Anne of the Thousand Days**

Inventions of 69 - The arpanet (first internet) invented, The artificial heart invented, The ATM invented, The bar-code scanner is invented.

1969 Calendar

January 1969

Sun	Mon	Tue	Wed	Thu	Fri	Sat
			1	2	3	4
5	6	7	8	9	10	11
12	13	14	15	16	17	18
19	20	21	22	23	24	25
26	27	28	29	30	31	

February 1969

Sun	Mon	Tue	Wed	Thu	Fri	Sat
						1
2	3	4	5	6	7	8
9	10	11	12	13	14	15
16	17	18	19	20	21	22
23	24	25	26	27	28	

March 1969

Sun	Mon	Tue	Wed	Thu	Fri	Sat
						1
2	3	4	5	6	7	8
9	10	11	12	13	14	15
16	17	18	19	20	21	22
23	24	25	26	27	28	29
30	31					

April 1969

Sun	Mon	Tue	Wed	Thu	Fri	Sat
		1	2	3	4	5
6	7	8	9	10	11	12
13	14	15	16	17	18	19
20	21	22	23	24	25	26
27	28	29	30			

May 1969

Sun	Mon	Tue	Wed	Thu	Fri	Sat
				1	2	3
4	5	6	7	8	9	10
11	12	13	14	15	16	17
18	19	20	21	22	23	24
25	26	27	28	29	30	31

June 1969

Sun	Mon	Tue	Wed	Thu	Fri	Sat
1	2	3	4	5	6	7
8	9	10	11	12	13	14
15	16	17	18	19	20	21
22	23	24	25	26	27	28
29	30					

July 1969

Sun	Mon	Tue	Wed	Thu	Fri	Sat
		1	2	3	4	5
6	7	8	9	10	11	12
13	14	15	16	17	18	19
20	21	22	23	24	25	26
27	28	29	30	31		

August 1969

Sun	Mon	Tue	Wed	Thu	Fri	Sat
					1	2
3	4	5	6	7	8	9
10	11	12	13	14	15	16
17	18	19	20	21	22	23
24	25	26	27	28	29	30
31						

September 1969

Sun	Mon	Tue	Wed	Thu	Fri	Sat
	1	2	3	4	5	6
7	8	9	10	11	12	13
14	15	16	17	18	19	20
21	22	23	24	25	26	27
28	29	30				

October 1969

Sun	Mon	Tue	Wed	Thu	Fri	Sat
			1	2	3	4
5	6	7	8	9	10	11
12	13	14	15	16	17	18
19	20	21	22	23	24	25
26	27	28	29	30	31	

November 1969

Sun	Mon	Tue	Wed	Thu	Fri	Sat
						1
2	3	4	5	6	7	8
9	10	11	12	13	14	15
16	17	18	19	20	21	22
23	24	25	26	27	28	29
30						

December 1969

Sun	Mon	Tue	Wed	Thu	Fri	Sat
	1	2	3	4	5	6
7	8	9	10	11	12	13
14	15	16	17	18	19	20
21	22	23	24	25	26	27
28	29	30	31			

Printed in Great Britain
by Amazon